Encounters with Silence

D0973850

Encounters with Silence

KARL RAHNER, S.J.

Translated by James M. Demske, S.J.

St. Augustine's Press
South Bend, Indiana
1999

Manufactured in the United States of America.

3 4 5 6   10 11 09 08 07 06

Library of Congress Cataloging in Publication Data
Rahner, Karl, 1904–
    [Worte ins Schweigen. English]
    Encounters with silence / Karl Rahner; translated by
    James M. Demske.
        p. cm.
    Originally published: Westminster, Md.: Newman
    Press, 1960.
    ISBN 1-890318-22-1 (pbk.: alk. paper)
    1. Devotional literature. I. Title.
    BX2184.R313 1999
    242—dc21   99-19018
                                                      CIP

∞ *The paper used in this publication meets the minimum
requirements of the American National Standard for
Information Sciences—Permanence of Paper for Printed
Materials, ANSI Z39.48-1984.*

Foreword

Karl Rahner, Professor of Dogmatic Theology at the University of Innsbruck in Austria, is one of the most influential Catholic theologians in Europe at the present time. His contributions have been highly esteemed not only by his Catholic confreres, but also in scholarly circles outside the Church.

The present work, a proof that his theology is as practical as it is profound, has met with great success on the Continent, having already gone through six editions in the original German, besides having been translated into Italian, Spanish, and French. It is hoped that it will aid likewise in a deepening of the spiritual life of the faithful in English-speaking lands.

THE TRANSLATOR

Contents

Encounters With Silence

CHAPTER I

God of My Life

I should like to speak with You, my God, and yet what else can I speak of but You? Indeed, could anything at all exist which had not been present with You from all eternity, which didn't have its true home and most intimate explanation in Your mind and heart? Isn't everything I ever say really a statement about You?

On the other hand, if I try, shyly and hesitantly, to speak to You about Yourself, You will still be hearing about *me*. For what could I say about You except that You are *my* God, the God of my beginning and end, God of my joy and my need, God of my life?

Of course You are endlessly more than merely the God of my life—if that's all You were, You wouldn't really be God at all. But even when I think of Your towering majesty, even when I acknowledge You as someone Who has no need of me, Who is infinitely far exalted above the lowly valleys through which I drag out the paths of my life—even then I have called You once again by the same name, God of my life.

And when I give praise to You as Father, Son, and

Holy Spirit, when I confess the thrice holy mystery of Your life, so eternally hidden in the abysses of Your Infinity that it leaves behind in creation no sign that we could make out by ourselves, am I not still praising You as the God of my life? Even granting that You had revealed to me this secret of Your own inner life, would I be able to accept and realize this mystery if *Your* life had not become *my* life through grace? Would I be able to acknowledge and love You, Father, and You, Eternal Word of the Father's Heart, and You, Spirit of the Father and the Son, if You had not deigned to become through grace the triune God of my life?

But what am I really saying, when I call You *my* God, the God of my life? That You are the meaning of my life? the goal of my wanderings? the consecration of my actions? the judgment of my sins? the bitterness of my bitter hours and my most secret joy? my strength, which turns *my own* strength into weakness? Creator, Sustainer, Pardoner, the One both far and near? Incomprehensible? God of my brethren? God of my fathers?

Are there any titles which I needn't give You? And when I have listed them all, what have I said? If I should take my stand on the shore of Your Endlessness and shout into the trackless reaches of Your Being all the words I have ever learned in the poor prison of my little existence, what should I have said? I should never have spoken the last word about You.

Then why do I even begin to speak of You? Why do You torment me with Your Infinity, if I can never really measure it? Why do You constrain me to walk along

4

Your paths, if they lead only to the awful darkness of Your night, where only You can see? For us, only the finite and tangible is real and near enough to touch: can You be real and near to me, when I must confess You as Infinite?

Why have You burnt Your mark in my soul in Baptism? Why have You kindled in me the flame of faith, this dark light which lures us out of the bright security of our little huts into Your night? And why have You made me Your priest, one whose vocation it is to be with You on behalf of men, when my finiteness makes me gasp for breath in Your presence?

Look at the vast majority of men, Lord—and excuse me if I presume to pass judgment on them—but do they often think of You? Are You the First Beginning and Last End for them, the One without whom their minds and hearts can find no rest? Don't they manage to get along perfectly well without You? Don't they feel quite at home in this world which they know so well, where they can be sure of just what they have to reckon with? Are You anything more for them than the One who sees to it that the world stays on its hinges, so that they won't have to call on You? Tell me, are You the God of *their* life?

I don't really know, Lord, if my complaint is just or not—who knows the heart of another man? You alone are the reader of hearts, O God, and how can I expect to understand the heart of another when I don't even understand my own? It's just that I can't help thinking of those others, because—as You well know, since You see into the depths of my heart, O Hidden God from whom nothing is

5

hidden—often enough I feel in myself a secret longing to be like them or, at least, to be as they seem to be.

O Lord, how helpless I am when I try to talk to You about Yourself! How can I call You anything but the God of my life? And what have I said with that title, when no name is really adequate? I'm constantly tempted to creep away from You in utter discouragement, back to the things that are more comprehensible, to things with which my heart feels so much more at home than it does with Your mysteriousness.

And yet, where shall I go? If the narrow hut of this earthly life with its dear, familiar trivialities, its joys and sorrows both great and small—if this were my real home, wouldn't it still be surrounded by Your distant Endlessness? Could the earth be my home without Your far-away heaven above it?

Suppose I tried to be satisfied with what so many today profess to be the purpose of their lives. Suppose I defiantly determined to admit my finiteness, and glory in it alone. I could only begin to recognize this finiteness and accept it as my sole destiny, because I had previously so often stared out into the vast reaches of limitless space, to those hazy horizons where Your Endless Life is just beginning.

Without You, I should founder helplessly in my own dull and groping narrowness. I could never feel the pain of longing, not even deliberately resign myself to being content with this world, had not my mind again and again soared out over its own limitations into the hushed reaches which are filled by You alone, the Silent Infinite. Where should I flee before You, when all my yearning for the unbounded, even my bold trust in my littleness, is really a confession of You?

What else is there that I can tell You about Yourself, except that You are the One without whom I cannot exist, the Eternal God from whom alone I, a creature of time, can draw the strength to live, the Infinity who gives meaning to my finiteness? And when I tell You all this, then I have given myself my true name, the name I ever repeat when I pray in David's Psalter, *"Tuus sum ego."* I am the one who belongs not to himself, but to You. I know no more than this about myself, nor about You, O God of my life, Infinity of my finiteness.

What a poor creature You have made me, O God! All I know about You and about myself is that You are the eternal mystery of my life. Lord, what a frightful puzzle man is! He belongs to You, and You are the Incomprehensible—Incomprehensible in Your Being, and even more-so in Your ways and judgments. For if all Your dealings with me are acts of Your freedom, quite unmerited gifts of Your grace which knows no "why," if my creation and my whole life hang absolutely on Your free decision, if all my paths are, after all, Your paths and, therefore, unsearchable, then, Lord, no amount of questioning will ever fathom Your depths—You will still be the Incomprehensible, even when I see You face to face.

But if You were not incomprehensible, You would be inferior to me, for my mind could grasp and assimilate You. You would belong to me, instead of I to You. And that would truly be hell, if I should belong only to myself! It would be the fate of the damned, to be doomed to pace up and down for all eternity in the cramped and confining prison of my own finiteness.

But can it be that You are my true home? Are You the One who will release me from my narrow little dungeon? Or are You merely adding another torment to my life, when You throw open the gates leading out upon Your broad and endless plain? Are You anything more than my own great insufficiency, if all my knowledge leads only to Your Incomprehensibility? Are You merely eternal unrest for the restless soul? Must every question fall dumb before You, unanswered? Is Your only response the mute "I will have it so," that so coldly smothers my burning desire to understand?

But I am rambling on like a fool—excuse me, O God. You have told me through Your Son that You are the God of my love, and You have commanded me to love You. Your commands are often hard because they enjoin the opposite of what my own inclinations would lead me to do, but when You bid me love You, You are ordering something that my own inclinations would never even dare to suggest: to love *You,* to come intimately close to You, to love Your very life. You ask me to lose myself in You, knowing that You will take me to Your Heart, where I may speak on loving, familiar terms with You, the incomprehensible mystery of my life. And all this because You are Love Itself.

Only in love can I find You, my God. In love the gates of my soul spring open, allowing me to breathe a new air of freedom and forget my own petty self. In love my whole being streams forth out of the rigid confines of

8

narrowness and anxious self-assertion, which make me a prisoner of my own poverty and emptiness. In love all the powers of my soul flow out toward You, wanting never more to return, but to lose themselves completely in You, since by Your love You are the inmost center of my heart, closer to me than I am to myself.

But when I love You, when I manage to break out of the narrow circle of self and leave behind the restless agony of unanswered questions, when my blinded eyes no longer look merely from afar and from the outside upon Your unapproachable brightness, and much more when You Yourself, O Incomprehensible One, have become through love the inmost center of my life, then I can bury myself entirely in You, O mysterious God, and with myself all my questions.

Love such as this wills to possess You as You are—how could it desire otherwise? It wants You Yourself, not Your reflection in the mirror of its own spirit. It wants to be united with You alone, so that in the very instant in which it gives up possession of itself, it will have not just Your image, but Your very Self.

Love wants You as You are, and just as love knows that it itself is right and good and needs no further justification, so You are right and good for it, and it embraces You without asking for any explanation of why You are as You are. Your "I will have it so" is love's greatest bliss. In this state of joy my mind no longer tries to bring You forcibly down to its level, in order to wrest from You Your eternal secret, but rather love seizes me and carries me up to Your level, into You.

When I abandon myself in love, then You are my very life, and Your Incomprehensibility is swallowed up in love's unity. When I am allowed to love You, the grasp of Your very mystery becomes a positive source of bliss. Then the farther Your Infinity is removed from my nothingness, the greater is the challenge to my love. The more complete the dependence of my fragile existence upon Your unsearchable counsels, the more unconditional must be the surrender of my whole being to You, beloved God. The more annihilating the incomprehensibility of Your ways and judgments, the greater must be the holy defiance of my love. And my love is all the greater and more blessed, the less my poor spirit understands of You.

God of my life, Incomprehensible, be my life. God of my faith, who lead me into Your darkness—God of my love, who turn Your darkness into the sweet light of my life, be now the God of my hope, so that You will one day be the God of my life, the life of eternal love.

CHAPTER II

God of My Lord Jesus Christ

Y ou are the Infinite, my God, the Limitless Being. Everything that is and can be is eternally present to You. Whatever I come to know has had its home in Your Mind from all eternity. Whatever I desire, You have always possessed. Whatever I love is fundamentally what Your Love has already eternally embraced, You Yourself. You are Wisdom, Power, Goodness, Life, and Strength. You are everything I can ever long for or imagine.

But how can You be all those things together? Here where I make my abode, the things that men know and love and long for are always separate, alienated from each other, dismembered. Things are limited—they have some qualities, but not others. Thought is pale and lifeless; goodness lacks power; power is without love; uncontrolled vitality turns deadly and brutal.

We never succeed in compressing together into the narrow confines of our finiteness everything that appears good to us, good just because it is: life and wisdom, goodness and power, strength and tenderness. These and all the other varied forces of our life are things we neither can nor want to do without, and yet each of them inevitably excludes another. There is only one thing we can do, and do it we must: order all these forces, arrange them in some kind of hierarchy, allot to each of them its proper place and limits, so that no single one becomes complete master and thus blots out all the others. We must preserve "order" in our life, we must live a life of "moderation."

We must be careful lest the spirit become the adversary of the soul, lest goodness turn into weakness, lest strength degenerate into mere brute force. All these things are like so many parasites clamoring for a share of our life's-blood, all greedily desiring to live in us and through us. And we must play the rôle of the thrifty housewife, parceling out our limited energy among them in tiny little measuring-cups.

There is nothing here into which we dare throw ourselves completely, nothing to which we can fully abandon ourselves. Any such lack of moderation would spell ruin both for us and for the object of our attachment. Those who know everything are seldom warm of heart; the mighty of this world are usually hard; and it is proverbial that the beautiful are often stupid. And so it must be: how could we be finite and be all these things together?

But where is All-Wisdom, which is also Eternal Love? All-Power, which remains All-Good? Pulsing Vitality, which is just as fully Living Spirit? Beauty, which is Vibrant and Wise? Where can these elements of greatness grow without limit, spread themselves irresistibly unto infinity? Where can they flourish and develop in such a

way that each still remains entirely compatible with everything else, in fact, is actually identified with everything else,
instead of pushing all the rest out of existence?

That Being is You, my God. You are all in all, and in
everything that You are, You are all. Each separate quality
that we attribute to You as something absolutely boundless,
instead of driving all other qualities out of the very realm
of possibility, rather gives them all limitless space for
development.

In You knowledge so expands itself to Omniscience
that it becomes Omnipotence, and the frightening in-
exorableness of Your Omnipotence turns into the irresist-
ible force of Your Goodness. All that is cramped and
confined, oppressed and imprisoned in the narrowness of
my finite being, becomes in You the one Infinity, which
is both Unity and Infinity combined. Each of Your attributes is of itself Your whole immeasurable Being; each
carries in its bosom the whole of reality. Thus, of all the
things man can love, there is at least one which he can
love without limit and unconditionally, without need for
"order" and "moderation," and that is You.

In loving Your holy Immensity, our ordinary life of
enforced moderation and proportion becomes tolerable.
In You the heart can safely follow its yearning for the
limitless, can wander aimlessly without going astray. I can
prodigally lavish my affections on every single aspect of
Your Being, and find in each of them everything I seek,
because everything in You is the whole.

When we find our way to You on this path of love,

then the burden of our finiteness is mercifully lifted from us, at least for the moment while such love lasts. And then we can come back to our dull daily routine and be satisfied again with the restrictions of our smallness.

Your Infinity, O God, is thus the salvation of our finiteness. And yet I must confess that the longer I think about You, the more anxious I become. Your Awful Being threatens my security, makes me lose all sense of direction. I am filled with fear and trembling because it often seems to me that Your Infinity, in which everything is really one and the same, is meant for You alone.

Obviously Your whole Being is present in each of Your attributes and in each of Your deeds. And You are also wholly present when You come down upon me, when You break into the circle of my life. You don't have to take any special measures to make sure that the lightning-stroke of Your Omnipotence, when it flashes across my life's horizon, is also the soft, gentle light of Your Wisdom.

You can channel Your whole Being into the torrent of Your Power, and all is still under control: the rushing waters have not gone beyond the limits You intended, have not released any new potentiality of which You Yourself are not the perfect fulfillment. You can be an inexorable tribunal of justice, and to Your ear a sentence of eternal damnation is still a hymn of joy praising Your immeasurable Goodness. But to me and my smallness that very thought brings terror—it makes me feel that all my joints are being sundered.

You are always Yourself, whole and entire, no matter

how You deal with me. You are always the Infinite Unity of all reality, whether You love me or pass over me, whether Your Power or Your Goodness, Your Justice or Your Mercy are revealed in me. But precisely because You are the one Infinity of all being and will always remain so no matter how You manifest Yourself, I am left in agonizing uncertainty. Whenever I think of Your Infinity, I am racked with anxiety, wondering how You are disposed toward me.

When I try to take You into account in the calculations of my life, I can only put You down as an "unknown" —the riddle of Your Infinity, which Itself contains everything, throws all my calculations off, and so the end result is still an insoluble puzzle. How can I use Your Goodness as a factor in my reckoning, when Goodness in You means also a holy severity? How can I add in Your fathomless Mercy, when it is also Your inexorable Justice? With this one word You tell me everything: Infinity. But it is precisely this word that renders futile all attempts at neatly planning out my life. You are thus the eternal threat in my life, frightening me out of all sense of security.

No, Lord, You must speak to me in a word that does not mean everything at once, a word that does not embrace the whole of reality in one unfathomable unity. You must say a word to me that means just one thing, one thing which is not everything. You must make Your infinite word finite, if I am to be spared this feeling of terror at Your Infinity.

You must adapt Your word to my smallness, so that it can enter into the tiny dwelling of my finiteness—the only dwelling in which I can live—without destroying it. Then I shall be able to understand; such a word I can take in without that agonizing bewilderment of mind and that cold fear clutching my heart. If You should speak such an "abbreviated" word, which would not say everything but only something simple which I could grasp, then I could breathe freely again.

You must make Your own some human word, for that's the only kind I can comprehend. Don't tell me everything that You are; don't tell me of Your Infinity— just say that You love me, just tell me of Your Goodness to me. But don't say this in Your divine language, in which Your Love also means Your inexorable Justice and Your crushing Power—say it rather in *my* language, so I won't have to be afraid that the word *love* hides some significance other than Your Goodness and gentle Mercy.

O Infinite God, You have actually willed to speak such a word to me! You have restrained the ocean of Your Infinity from flooding in over the poor little wall which protects my tiny life's-acre from Your Vastness. Not the waters of Your great sea, but only the dew of Your Gentleness is to spread itself over my poor little plot of earth. You have come to me in a human word. For You, the Infinite, are the God of Our Lord Jesus Christ.

He has spoken to us in human language. No more can the word *love* mean anything that I must fear. For when He says that He loves us, and that in Him You love us, this word comes from a human heart. And to a human heart this word has only one meaning, only one blessed and blissful meaning. If this human heart loves us, the heart

of Your Son, the heart which—may You be praised forever!—is finite like my own poor heart, then my heart is at
peace. For it loves me, and I know that such a love is
only love and nothing else.

Jesus has really told me that He loves me, and His
word has come from the depths of His human heart. And
His heart is Your heart, O God of Our Lord Jesus Christ.
Thus, if this human heart of Your Son is unspeakably
richer and greater than my heart, it is so only in that love
and that goodness which can never be anything else but
love and goodness. It can never conceal within itself the
awe-fulness of Your Infinity, which is always all else as
well.

Grant, O Infinite God, that I may ever cling fast to
Jesus Christ, my Lord. Let His heart reveal to me how You
are disposed toward me. I shall look upon His heart when I
desire to know Who You are. The eye of my mind is
blinded whenever it looks only at Your Infinity, in which
You are totally present in each and every aspect at once.
Then I am surrounded by the darkness of Your unbound-
edness, which is harsher than all my earthly nights. But
instead I shall gaze upon His human heart, O God of Our
Lord Jesus Christ, and then I shall be sure that You
love me.

But I have still one more request. Make my heart like
that of Your Son. Make it as great and rich in love as His,
so that my brothers—or at least one of them, sometime in
my life—can enter through this door and there learn that
You love him. God of Our Lord Jesus Christ, let me find
You in His heart.

CHAPTER III

God of My Prayer

I should like to speak with You about my prayer, O Lord. And though it often seems to me that You pay little heed to what I try to say to You in my prayers, please listen to me carefully now.

O Lord God, I don't wonder that my prayers fall so short of You—even I myself often fail to pay the least bit of attention to what I'm praying about. So often I consider my prayer as just a job I have to do, a duty to be performed. I "get it out of the way" and then relax, glad to have it behind me. When I'm at prayer, I'm at my "duty," instead of being with You.

Yes, that's my prayer. I admit it. And yet, my God, I find it hard to be sorry for praying so poorly. How can a man hope to speak with You? You are so distant and so mysterious. When I pray, it's as if my words have disappeared down some deep, dark well, from which no echo ever comes back to reassure me that they have struck the ground of Your heart.

Lord, to pray my whole life long without hearing an answer, isn't that too much to ask? You see how I run away from You time and time again, to speak with men who give me an answer, to busy myself with things that give me some kind of response. You see how much I *need* to be answered. And yet, my prayers never receive a word of reply. Or should I say that the interior motion that comes to me in prayer, the occasional light I receive in meditation, is Your word, Your enlightenment? This, of course, is the pat and ready answer which pious writers are so eager to give. But I find it very hard to believe. Again and again I find only myself in all these experiences, only the empty echo of my own cry, when it's Your word, You Yourself, that I want to hear.

I and my ideas are at most useful to me for the sake of others, even when these ideas concern You, and when people think they're quite profound. I shudder at my "profundity," which is really only the flatness of a human being, and a very ordinary one at that. And an "inwardness" in which one finds only himself leaves the heart even more empty than any dissipation or abandonment to the idle bustle of the world.

I find myself endurable only when I can forget myself, when I can get away from myself by prayer and find life in You. But how can I do this if You never show Yourself to me, if You remain ever so distant? Why are You so silent? Why do You enjoin me to speak with You, when You don't pay any attention to me? Isn't Your silence a sure sign that You're not listening?

Or do You really listen quite attentively, do You perhaps listen my whole life long, until I have told You everything, until I have spoken out my entire self to You?

Do You remain so silent precisely because You are waiting until I am really finished, so that You can then speak Your word to me, the word of Your eternity? Are you silent so that You can one day bring to a close the life-long monologue of a poor human being, burdened by the darkness of this world, by speaking the luminous word of eternal life, in which You will express Your very Self in the depths of my heart?

Is my life really no more than a single short aspiration, and all my prayers just different formulations of it in human words? Is the eternal possession of You Your eternal answer to it? Is Your silence when I pray really a discourse filled with infinite promise, unimaginably more meaningful than any audible word You could speak to the limited understanding of my narrow heart, a word that would itself have to become as small and poor as I am?

I suppose that's the way it is, Lord. But if that is Your answer to my complaint—in case You should choose to answer me at all—then I am ready with still another objection, and this one comes from an even more anguished heart than my complaint at Your silence, O my distant God.

If my life is supposed to be one single prayer, and my praying is to be a part of this life carried on humbly in Your presence, then I must have the power to present my life, my very self before You. But this is completely beyond my strength.

When I pray, my mouth does the speaking and, if I am praying "well," my thoughts and will-acts obediently play their required, well-memorized little rôle. But is it I myself who constitute the object of the prayer? After all, I'm not supposed to be praying just words or thoughts or will-acts, but *myself*—I should be putting my "self" into my prayer. Even my will belongs far too much to the surface of my soul, and is far too weak to penetrate into those deep levels of my being where I am really "I," where the hidden waters of my life rise and fall according to their own unique law.

What little power I have over myself! Do I really love You when I *want* to love You? Love is a complete pouring out of oneself, a total clinging from the last depths of one's being. Is this what I mean when I say I want to love You?

How can I pray with love, when the prayer of love is the absolute surrender of the heart from its deepest roots, the throwing open of the inmost sanctuary of the soul? I don't have the strength even to budge the heavy gates of this sanctuary—I can only stand helpless and feeble before the ultimate mystery of myself, a mystery which lies buried, immovable and unapproachable, in depths beyond the reach of my ordinary freedom.

I know, my God, that my prayer need not be enthusiastic and ecstatic to succeed in placing me so much in Your power and at Your disposal that nothing is held back from You. Prayer can be real prayer, even when it is not filled with bliss and jubilation or the shining brilliance of a carefree surrender of self. Prayer can be like a slow interior bleeding, in which grief and sorrow make the heart's-blood of the inner man trickle away silently into his own unfathomed depths.

It would be all right if I could pray in this way, or in that other way, if I were just able to give You in prayer the only thing You want: not my thoughts and feelings and resolutions, but myself. But that's just what I am unable to do, because in the superficiality of the ordinary routine into which my life is cast, I am a stranger even to myself. And how can I seek You, O distant God, how can I give myself up to You, when I haven't even been able as yet to find myself?

Be merciful to me, my God. When I flee from prayer, it's not that I want to flee from You, but from myself and my own superficiality. I don't want to run away from Your Infinity and Holiness, but from the deserted market-place of my own soul. Every time I try to pray, I am doomed to wander in the barren wastes of my own emptiness, since I have left the world behind, and still cannot find my way into the true sanctuary of my inner self, the only place where You can be found and adored.

Doesn't Your loving sympathy make You understand that, when I am shut out from the place where You live and banned to the market place before Your cathedral, I unfortunately fill up this market with the busy distractions of the world? Doesn't Your mercy make You understand that the empty clatter of these distractions is far sweeter to me than the grim and forbidding stillness when I try to pray? This awful quiet is the sole result of my futile efforts at prayer, since I deliberately shut out the noises of the world, and yet I am still hopelessly deaf to the eloquent sounds of Your silence.

23

What shall I do? You have commanded me to pray, and how can I believe that You have commanded something impossible? I believe that You have given me the order to pray and that I can carry it out with Your grace. And since that's so, the prayer that You require of me must be ultimately just a patient waiting for You, a silent standing by until You, who are ever present in the inmost center of my being, open the gate to me from within. In this way I shall be able to enter into myself, into the hidden sanctuary of my own being, and there, at least once in my life, empty out before You the vessel of my heart's-blood. That will be the true hour of *my* love.

Whether this hour comes in a time of "prayer" in its ordinary meaning, or in some other hour of decision affecting my soul's salvation, or at the time of my death—whether it will be clearly recognizable as *the* hour of my life or not—whether it will last a long time or only a moment—all that is known to You alone. But I must stand ever ready and waiting, so that when You open the door to the decisive moment of my life—and maybe You'll do it very quietly and inconspicuously—I shall not be so taken up with the affairs of this world that I miss the one great opportunity to enter into myself and into You. Then in my trembling hands I shall hold "myself," that nameless something in which all my powers and qualities are united as in their source, and I shall return this nameless thing to You in an offering of love.

I know not whether this hour has already struck in my life. I only know that its last moment will be the moment of my death. In that blessed and terrible hour You will still be silent. You will still let me do all the talking, speaking out my own self to You.

Theologians call Your silence in such a decisive hour the "dark night of the soul," and those who have experienced it are "mystics." These are the great souls who have not merely "lived through" this hour of decision, as all men must, but have been able to watch themselves in the process, to be somehow witnesses of their own reactions.

And after this moment shall have come for me, after the hour of *my* love, which is shrouded in Your silence, then will come the endless day of *Your* love, the eternity of the beatific vision. But for now, since I don't know when my hour is coming, nor whether it has already begun to come or not, I must just wait in the courtyard before Your sanctuary and mine. I must empty it of all the noise of the world, and quietly endure the bitter silence and desolation thus produced—the terrible "night of the senses"—in Your grace and in pure faith.

This, then, is the ultimate meaning of my daily prayers, this awful waiting. It's not what I feel or think of in them, not the resolutions I make, not any superficial activity of my mind and will that You find pleasing in my prayer. All that is only the fulfillment of a command and, at the same time, the free gift of Your grace. All that is only clearing the ground, so the soul will be ready for that precious moment when You offer it the possibility of losing itself in the finding of You, of praying itself into You.

Give me, O God of my prayer, the grace to continue waiting for You in prayer.

CHAPTER IV

God of Knowledge

How many things have passed through my brain in the course of my life, O my God! How many things have I thought and learned!

Not as though I now knew them all. I have learned much because I had to, much because I wanted to, but in either case the end result was always the same: I forgot it again. It slipped away from me because our poor, narrow human minds simply cannot take in and hold one thing without letting another sink into oblivion. Or maybe it slipped away because in the very learning of it, there was a hidden indifference which prevented its becoming anything more than another object of bored acceptance and eventual forgetting.

At any rate, most of what I have learned, I have learned in order to forget it again and thus to experience concretely, even in the area of knowledge, my own poverty, narrowness, and limitation. No, that *in order to* is no grammatical mistake or flaw in logic. For look, Lord: if the forgetting were only a tragic mishap and not the true and proper end of all my learning and knowledge, then I would have to desire to know everything I had ever learned.

What a horrible thought! I would still have to retain all the things that were ever crammed into me in all the subjects I ever studied at school. I would still know everything I had ever heard in idle conversations, all I had ever seen in foreign lands or gawked at in museums. And what good would it all do me? Would I be any richer, any more developed or refined?

How could I ever retain it all, anyway? Would it be all stored up in memory like items in a warehouse, to be taken down from the shelf every time an order came in? Or, in the ideal case, would all these items of knowledge be consciously present to me at once?

But how could this vast, confused swarm of knowledge possibly be of any use to me? What would I ever need it for? To make use of it all, I should have to live my whole life over again, right from the first glimmer of consciousness.

O God, it's good to forget. In fact, the best part of most of the things I once knew is precisely the fact that they could be forgotten. Without protest, they have sunk gently and peacefully out of sight. And thus they have enabled me literally to see through them in all their inner poverty and ultimate insignificance.

It is said—and who am I to dispute it, Lord?—that knowing belongs to the highest part of man, to the most properly human of all his actions. And You Yourself are called *"Deus scientiarum Dominus,"* the Lord God of all knowledge. But doesn't such high praise contradict the experience of Your holy writer? "I applied my mind to a new study; what meant wisdom and learning, what meant ignorance and folly? And I found that this too was labor lost; much wisdom, much woe; who adds to learning, adds to the load we bear" (Ecclus. 1:17–18).

It is also said that knowing is the most interior way of grasping and possessing anything. But actually it seems to me that knowing touches only the surface of things, that it fails to penetrate to the heart, to the depths of my being where I am most truly "I."

Knowledge seems more like a kind of pain-killing drug that I have to take repeatedly against the boredom and desolation of my heart. And no matter how faithful I may be to it, it can never really cure me. All it can give me is words and concepts, which perform the middle-man's service of expressing and interpreting reality to me, but can never still my heart's craving for the reality itself, for true life and true possession. I shall never be cured until all reality comes streaming like an ecstatic, intoxi-cating melody into my heart.

Truly, my God, mere knowing is nothing. All it can give us is the sad realization of its own inadequacy. All it can tell us is that through it we can never fully grasp reality and make it a living part of ourselves.

How can we approach the heart of all things, the true heart of reality? Not by knowledge alone, but by the full flower of knowledge, love. Only the experience of knowl-edge's blooming into love has any power to work a trans-formation in me, in my very self. For it is only when I am fully present to an object that I am changed by meeting it.

And it is only in love that I am fully present—not in bare knowing, but in the affection engendered by knowing. Only then is my knowledge anything more than a fleeting shadow, passing across the stage of consciousness. Then I have knowledge which is really myself, which abides as I myself abide.

Only knowledge gained through experience, the fruit of living and suffering, fills the heart with the wisdom of love, instead of crushing it with the disappointment of boredom and final oblivion. It is not the results of our own speculation, but the golden harvest of what we have lived through and suffered through, that has power to enrich the heart and nourish the spirit. And all the knowledge we have acquired through study can do no more than give us some little help in meeting the problems of life with an alert and ready mind.

Thanks to Your mercy, O Infinite God, I know something about You not only through concepts and words, but through experience. I have actually known You through living contact; I have met You in joy and suffering. For You are the first and last experience of my life. Yes, really You Yourself, not just a concept of You, not just the name which we ourselves have given You! You have descended upon me in water and the Spirit, in my baptism. And then there was no question of my contriving or excogitating anything about You. Then my reason with its extravagant cleverness was still silent. Then, without asking me, You made Yourself my poor heart's destiny.

You have seized me; I have not "grasped" You. You have transformed my being right down to its very last roots and made me a sharer in Your own Being and Life. You have given me Yourself, not just a distant, fuzzy report of Yourself in human words. And that's why I can never forget You, because You have become the very center of my being.

Now that You live in me, my spirit is filled with something more than pale, empty words about reality, words whose tremendous variety and prolific confusion serve only to perplex and weary me. In baptism, Father, You have spoken Your Word into my being, the Word that was before all things and is more real than they are, the Word in which all reality and all life subsists, endures, and has its being.

This Word, in which alone is life, has become my experience through your action, O God of Grace. Of Him I shall never tire, because He is one and yet infinite. He can never become tedious or boresome to me, because He is eternal. He draws my spirit away from constant change and inconstancy into a realm of peace, where I experience the ever-old and ever-new possession of everything in one.

Your Word and Your Wisdom is in me, not because I comprehend You with my understanding, but because I have been recognized by You as Your son and friend. Of course, this Word, born as it is out of Your own Heart and marvelously spoken into mine, must still be explained to me through the external word that I have accepted in faith, the "faith through hearing" of which St. Paul speaks.

Your living Word is still shrouded in darkness. It still echoes ever so faintly from the depths of my heart, where You have spoken it, up into the foreground of consciousness, where my scrawny knowledge is wont to parade and take itself so seriously. This is the knowledge that ends in despondency and agony of soul, that brings nothing but the bitter experience of being forgotten and of deserving to be forgotten, because it can never produce living, organic unity. And yet, behind all this labor and torment there is already another "knowledge," which has become in me grace-filled reality: Your Word and Your Eternal Light.

Oh, grow in me, enlighten me, shine forth ever stronger in me, eternal Light, sweet Light of my soul. Sound out in me ever more clearly, O Word of the Father, Word of Love, Jesus. You've said that You have revealed to us all You have heard from the Father. And Your word is true, for what You have heard from the Father is You Yourself, O Word of the Father. You are the Word which knows Itself and the Father. And You are mine, O Word beyond all human words, O Light before whom all earthly light is only night's blackness.

May You alone enlighten me, You alone speak to me. May all that I know apart from You be nothing more than a chance traveling companion on the journey toward You. May it help to mature me, so that I may ever better understand You in the suffering that it brings me, as Your holy writer has predicted. When it has accomplished this, then it can quietly disappear into oblivion.

Then You will be the final Word, the only one that remains, the one we shall never forget. Then at last, everything will be quiet in death; then I shall have finished with all my learning and suffering. Then will begin the great silence, in which no other sound will be heard but You, O Word resounding from eternity to eternity.

Then all human words will have grown dumb. Being and knowing, understanding and experience will have become one and the same. "I shall know even as I am known"; I shall understand what You have been saying to me all along, namely, You Yourself. No more human words, no more concepts, no more pictures will stand between us. You Yourself will be the one exultant word of love and life filling out every corner of my soul.

Be now my consolation, O Lord, now when all knowledge, even Your revelation expressed in human language, fails to still the yearning of my heart. Give me strength, O God, now when my soul easily tires of all the human words we devise about You, words which still fail to give us the possession of You. Even though the few flashes of light I receive in quiet moments quickly fade out again into the dark-grey sky of my daily life—even though knowledge comes to me now only to sink back again into oblivion, still Your Word lives in me, of which it is written: "The Word of the Lord abides forever."

You Yourself are my knowledge, the knowledge that is light and life. You Yourself are my knowledge, experience, and love. You are the God of the one and only knowledge that is eternal, the knowledge that is bliss without end.

CHAPTER V

God of Law

In Your book it is written of You, O God, that You are Spirit, and Your Holy Spirit is called the Spirit of freedom: "The Lord is Spirit; and where the Spirit of the Lord is, there is freedom" (2 Cor. 3:17). And this is said of You not in the sense that You reign absolutely free and sovereign in the boundless expanses of Your own life, but in the sense that You are *our* spirit and *our* life.

O God of freedom, our God, it sometimes seems to me that we believe this truth of You because we feel ourselves bound to it by the law of faith. We acknowledge You as our God of freedom because we must, and not so much because the sweeping exuberance of Your Life has filled our hearts, and Your rushing Spirit, who blows wherever He will, has made us free.

Are You truly the Spirit of freedom in my life, or are You not rather the God of law? Or are You both? Are you perhaps the God of freedom through law? Your laws, which You Yourself have given us, are not chains—Your commands are commands of freedom. In their austere and inexorable simplicity they set us free from our own dull narrowness, from the drag of our pitiful, cowardly concupiscence. They awaken in us the freedom of loving You.

Your commands are also truth, since they order us to put first things first, and forbid us to enthrone baseness upon the altar of our life. And since they are truth, they set us free, these commands which You Yourself have given in the New Covenant, or rather have left to us when you abrogated the Old Law, when Christ "freed us unto freedom" (Gal. 5:1). Now nothing more remains for us but "the law of freedom" (Jas. 2:12). Your commandments may be hard, but they set us free.

But, Lord, what of the commandments imposed upon us by men, issued in Your name? Let me tell you quite frankly what rumbles through my heart when the spirit of criticism and discontent is upon me, O God of freedom and of sincere, open speech. I can tell you with confidence —You listen indulgently to such things.

Lord, You have abrogated the Old Law, "which neither our fathers nor we have been able to bear" (Acts 15:10). But You have established rulers in this world, both temporal and spiritual, and sometimes it seems to me that they have diligently set about patching up all the holes that Your Spirit of freedom had torn in the fence of rules and regulations by His liberating Pentecostal storm.

First there are the 2414 paragraphs of the Church's law-book. And even these haven't sufficed: how many "responsa" to inquiries have been added to bring joy to the hearts of the jurists! And then there are several thousand liturgical decrees clamoring for our attention. In order to praise You in the Breviary "in psalms and hymns and spiritual songs," in order to "sing and make melody in the heart" (Eph. 5:19), I need a road map, a *directorium,* so intricate and elaborate that it requires a new edition every year!

Then there are also various "official bulletins" in the Kingdom of Your Holy Spirit, not to mention countless files, inquiries, replies, reports, decisions, meetings, citations, instructions from every kind of Congregation and Commission. And how resourceful the moralists are at asking tricky questions, until all the pronouncements of all higher authorities are neatly ordered and interpreted.

And what delicate calculations must go into the granting of an indulgence! Only recently some learned theologians found occasion to dispute whether a sick person is obliged to kiss the crucifix of Your Son fourteen times or six times, or less, in order to gain an indulgence. What incredible zeal Your servants and stewards have shown in Your absence, during the long period while You have been away on your journey into the distant silence of eternity! And yet, according to Your own word, where the Spirit of the Lord is, there is freedom.

I don't mean to accuse them, Lord, these wise and faithful servants whom you have placed over Your household. Rather I must say to their praise that they are usually not vulnerable to the reproach which Your Son once made against the Scribes and Pharisees who sat upon the chair of Moses (Matt. 23:4). Unlike those rulers and teachers of old, Your modern stewards have imposed heavy burdens not only on others, but on themselves too.

Generally speaking, Lord, Your household of the laity

has only Your sweet yoke and Your light burden to carry, belief in Your Word, Your own commandment that frees us unto love, and the burden of Your grace flowing from the sacraments. And if this yoke weighs heavily upon us, then it's only because we're weak and our hearts are evil, so that we should actually complain against ourselves and not against Your yoke. The burden about which I was complaining in the stillness of my heart is mainly *our* burden, the burden of Your priests, which we have actually picked up and set upon our own shoulders.

But isn't it still a real burden? Or is it only Your kind of freedom, which seems heavy and constraining to our narrow, petty, comfort-seeking hearts? Is it only the excess weight of Your grace? There is perhaps no more enlightened or enlightening answer to this question than that given by Your Son. He has told us that Your lower servants should do and observe all that Your higher servants have commanded them, and that those to whom You have given power to bind and loose must one day give an accounting to You, as to whether their binding was always really a releasing of their brethren into the realm of Your true freedom (Matt. 23:3).

I know, and I hope that this knowledge will grow ever stronger and more vital in me, that Your freedom can never be won through protest against the authorities who derive their power from You. We can transform that weighty power into Your buoyant freedom only by doing what is right, only by using it as "Your minister for good" (Rom. 13:3-4).

When I am really honest with myself, I recognize time

and time again that it is not Your Holy Spirit of freedom that makes this burden so vexing, but the unholy spirit of my own love of comfort, my own self-will and self-seeking. I rise up in rebellion because I will not take the trouble to have consideration for my brother, to avoid scandalizing him, even though I know that Your Son shed His Blood for him; because I want to consider everything that is clean as allowed; because I have the knowledge which puffs up, and not the charity which edifies (Rom. 14:13 ff.; 1 Cor. 8:1 ff.).

And haven't I often called things barriers and restrictions upon Your freedom, when they were actually a defensive wall for the protection of the liberty of loving You, a safeguard against the law in my own members? How many times have I learned through hard experience that the human laws of Your Church are a salutary school of patience and discipline, of self-mastery and self-possession, of consideration and love of neighbor?

How often have I found out that we grow to maturity not by doing what we like, but by doing what we should? How true it is that not every *should* is a compulsion, and not every *like* is high morality and true freedom. Conscious willing is found even in infants, but consciously accepted obligation is the sign of a mature man. O grant that I may not always belong to the class of the infants who continually want to play the game differently, who are never satisfied with the rules as they are!

I know too that all the detailed rules and regulations, the ceremonies and customs, methods and tricks of the trade which are commanded, or at least recommended to

39

me, can be made the external expression of my interior love, provided of course that I have the love. I know that these things are dead weight only when I myself am too weak and lifeless to put my heart into them.

Your Church, O my God, has to be visible. Only thus is she the "vessel of the Holy Spirit," as Irenaeus called her. And if she is to be visible, if Your Spirit is to become ever more visible and tangible in her, then she must express herself in commandments and customs, in "yes and no," in "here and now," in "thus and not otherwise." And he who grasps all this with a believing heart and a vigorous love, enters through the narrow gate of the commandments into the broad expanse of Your Spirit.

O my God, I have talked much to prove my good will toward the many commandments and orders, and the even more numerous prohibitions of the spiritual authorities that you have set over me. I want to observe all that they have commanded. And this will definitely be a blessing to me. But what of You Yourself: are You the God of these laws?

Obviously You want me to keep them: that much is clear. And it's also clear that, in order to understand Your will properly, we must keep in mind several of the things that the moralists say at the beginning of their books about norms of interpretation, causes excusing from culpability, canonical equity, etc. But are You really the God of such laws?

It's hard for me to make clear, even to myself, what I mean by this question. Let me put it this way: in the commandments which You Yourself have given, it's almost

as if You were actually present. You have made them
Your commandments, precisely because that which they
contain is the expression of Your own Holiness and Goodness, because we would be unlike You if we did not love
what You command. Our rejection of Your commandments would be ultimately a rejection of You Yourself.

But it's not like that in the case of the laws originating
from human authority. The prescribed cut of the clerical
gown in itself has nothing to do with the Holiness of
Your Being—I can serve You as a priest no matter how
long or short a cassock I wear. You are not present in
that law, just as you would not be present in its opposite.
Why, then, must I seek You in precisely this way, when
You could just as well be found in another?

Is it because the authorities You have placed over me
have so ordered? Yes, of course. But why must they order
precisely this? Because the unbounded realm of the possible can be reduced to living actuality only by a more or
less arbitrary choice? Because otherwise, if everyone were
free to choose according to his own arbitrary judgment,
there would arise disorder and hopeless confusion? Yes,
that may often enough be the reason. But is it the reason
always and in every case? Can all the laws and regulations
of Your Kingdom be considered merely as necessary ordinances insuring order and uniformity, as mere concrete
determinations of Your own Law? Are they only spiritual
traffic laws?

If they were no more than this, then they would constitute no burden to our inner, personal freedom. No one
can seriously claim that his personal liberty is unduly

restricted by traffic laws. But what of the other laws, which are not simply concrete expressions of Your own Law, and yet are something more than mere external regulations governing the area of interpersonal relations? What of these, which affect me interiorly, in my own personal being and its freedom?

I am not asking You whether I should obey these laws —the answer to that question is perfectly clear to me— but rather how I can obey them in such a way that I meet You in them. It's true: they require my interior compliance, and not just external fulfillment, since they govern my inner self, directing the personal actions of the real "me." And yet they are not like Your own commandments, for when I obey these, I can be confident that my subjection to the law is *eo ipso* an act of devotion to You.

I always feel that, if one is not careful, he can easily become a mere fulfiller of the law, doing what is commanded externally and quite apathetically. He can turn into a "legalist," an anxious, slavish worshiper of the letter of the law, who thinks he has fulfilled all justice before You when he has fulfilled the human ordinance. Such a man mistakes the letter of the law for You Yourself.

I don't want to be a legalist, nor a mere servant of men, nor a servant of the dead letter. And still I must fulfill the commands of human superiors. I want to observe their ordinances with all my heart, but I can't see how I can give my heart completely to such an object. The inner man should obey such laws, and yet he should not be a slave of men.

Thus, the only answer seems to be that, whenever I

obey such a law, I must keep looking directly at You. In this way I can pay homage to You, directly and exclusively, and not to the thing that is required of me, not even to the thing as the reflected splendor of Your Being. Precisely because there is in the thing itself nothing to which I can give my heart without reserve, obedience can be the expression of my seeking You alone in it.

Thus, in obedience to such human regulations, either I don't find You at all, or I find You and You alone, according as I obey out of pure love of You or not. In Your own commandments You are present even when we obey them without intending our obedience as an act of love of You, because their very content is necessarily an expression of Your sacred Being. But in the commandments of human superiors we find nothing but a human will, and thus, instead of making us free, they take away freedom, unless we obey them out of love of You.

If I look upon my obedience to these human laws as a demonstration of homage for Your beloved free Will, which rules over me according to its own good pleasure, then I can truly find You therein. Then my whole being flows toward You, into You, into the broad, free expanse of Your unbounded Being, instead of being cramped within the narrow confines of human orders. You are the God of human laws for me, only when You are the God of my love.

Give me a ready and willing heart, O Lord. Let me bear the burden of the commands issued by Your authorities in such a way that this bearing is an exercise of selflessness, of patience, of fidelity. Give me Your Love, which is the only true freedom, the love without which all obedience to human authority is mere external observance and servitude. Give me a heart filled with reverence for every legitimate command, and also respect for the freedom of Your children, which You have won for me by Your own redeeming obedience.

May the kingdom of Your freedom come! It is the kingdom of Your Love, and it is only there that I am truly free from myself and from the will of my fellow men, because there I am not serving them, nor for their sakes, but serving You, for Your sake.

In no command do I belong to men, but to You, and he who belongs to You is free. You are not the God of laws because You will that we should serve the law: You are rather the God of the one law, that we should give our love and service to You alone.

And I pray also, as You wish me to pray, for all superiors You have placed over me, that their commands may never be anything else but the appearance and fulfillment on earth of the one great law of loving You.

CHAPTER VI

God of My Daily Routine

I should like to bring the routine of my daily life before You, O Lord, to discuss the long days and tedious hours that are filled with everything else but You.

Look at this routine, O God of Mildness. Look upon us men, who are practically nothing else but routine. In Your loving mercy, look at my soul, a road crowded by a dense and endless column of bedraggled refugees, a bomb-pocked highway on which countless trivialities, much empty talk and pointless activity, idle curiosity and ludicrous pretensions of importance all roll forward in a never-ending stream.

When it stands before You and Your infallible Truthfulness, doesn't my soul look just like a market place where the second-hand dealers from all corners of the globe have assembled to sell the shabby riches of this world? Isn't it just like a noisy bazaar, where I and the rest of mankind display our cheap trinkets to the restless, milling crowds?

Many years ago, when I was a schoolboy distinguished by the name of "philosopher," I learned that the soul is somehow everything. O God, how the meaning of that lofty-sounding phrase has changed! How different it sounds to me now, when my soul has become a huge warehouse where day after day the trucks unload their crates without any plan or discrimination, to be piled helterskelter in every available corner and cranny, until it is crammed full from top to bottom with the trite, the commonplace, the insignificant, the routine.

What will become of me, dear God, if my life goes on like this? What will happen to me when all the crates are suddenly swept out of the warehouse? How will I feel at the hour of my death? Then there will be no more "daily routine"; then I shall suddenly be abandoned by all the things that now fill up my days here on earth.

And what will I myself be at that hour, when I am only myself and nothing else? My whole life long I have been nothing but the ordinary routine, all business and activity, a desert filled with empty sound and meaningless fury. But when the heavy weight of death one day presses down upon my life and squeezes the true and lasting content out of all those many days and long years, what will be the final yield?

Maybe at that last reckoning, at the time of the great disillusionment that will take the place of the great illusion of my tritely spent earthly life, maybe then, O God, if you have been merciful to me, the genuine yield of my ungenuine life will be only a few blessed moments, made luminous and living by Your grace. Maybe then I shall see the few precious instants when the grace of Your Love has succeeded in stealing into an obscure corner of my life, in between the countless bales of second-hand goods that fill up my everyday routine.

How can I redeem this wretched humdrum? How can I turn myself toward the one thing necessary, toward You? How can I escape from the prison of this routine? Haven't You Yourself committed me to it? And didn't I find myself already in exile, from the very first moment I began to realize that my true life must be directed toward You? Wasn't I already deeply entangled in the pettiness of everyday cares, when it first dawned on me that I must not allow myself to be suffocated under the weight of earthly routine?

Aren't You my Creator? Haven't You made me a human being? And what is man but a being that is not sufficient to itself, a being who sees his own insufficiency, so that he longs naturally and necessarily for Your Infinity? What is man but the being who must follow the urge to run toward Your distant stars, who must keep up his chase until he has covered all the highways and byways of this world, only in the end to see your stars still coursing their serenely ordered way—and as far away as ever?

Even if I should try to escape from my routine by becoming a Carthusian, so that I'd have nothing more to do but spend my days in silent adoration of Your holy presence, would that solve my problem? Would that really lift me out of my rut?

I'm afraid not, since not even the sacred actions I now perform are free from the corrosive dust of this spirit of

47

routine. When I think of all the hours I have spent at Your holy altar, or reciting Your Church's official prayer in my Breviary, then it becomes clear to me that I myself am responsible for making my life so humdrum. It's not the affairs of the world that make my days dull and insignificant; I myself have dug the rut. Through my own attitude I can transform the holiest events into the grey tedium of dull routine. My days don't make *me* dull—it's the other way around.

That's why I now see clearly that, if there is any path at all on which I can approach You, it must lead through the very middle of my ordinary daily life. If I should try to flee to You by any other way, I'd actually be leaving myself behind, and that, aside from being quite impossible, would accomplish nothing at all.

But is there a path through my daily life that leads to You? Doesn't this road take me ever farther away from You? Doesn't it immerse me all the more deeply in the empty noise of worldly activity, where You, God of Quiet, do not dwell?

I realize that we gradually get tired of the feverish activity that seems so important to a young mind and heart. I know that the *taedium vitae,* of which the moral philosophers speak, and the feeling of satiety with life, which Your Scripture reports as the final earthly experience of Your patriarchs, will also become more and more my own lot. My daily routine will automatically turn into the great melancholy of life, thus indirectly leading me to You, the infinite counterpart of this earthly emptiness.

But I don't have to be a Christian to know that—don't

the pagans experience it too? Is this the way my every-day life is supposed to lead to You? Do I come into Your presence just because this life has revealed its true face to me, finally admitting that all is vanity, all is misery?

Isn't that the road to despair rather than the way to You? Isn't it the crowning victory for routine, when a man's burned-out heart no longer finds the least bit of joy in things that formerly gave him relief, when even the simple things of his ordinary life, which he used to be able to call upon to help him over the periods of bore-dom and emptiness, have now become tasteless to him?

Is a tired and disillusioned heart any closer to You than a young and happy one? Where can we ever hope to find You, if neither our simple joys nor ordinary sorrows suc-ceed in revealing You to us? Indeed our day-to-day pleas-ures seem somehow especially designed to make us forget about You, and with our daily disappointments it's no better: they make our hearts so sick and bitter that we seem to lose any talent we ever had for discovering You.

O God, it seems we can lose sight of You in anything we do. Not even prayer, or the Holy Sacrifice, or the quiet of the cloister, not even the great disillusion with life itself can fully safeguard us from this danger. And thus it's clear that even these sacred, non-routine things belong ultimately to our routine. It's evident that routine is not just a part of my life, not even just the greatest part, but the whole. *Every* day is "everyday." Everything I do is routine, be-cause everything can rob me of the one and only thing I really need, which is You, my God.

But on the other hand, if it's true that I can lose You

in everything, it must also be true that I can find You in everything. If You have given me no single place to which I can flee and be sure of finding You, if anything I do can mean the loss of You, then I must be able to find You in every place, in each and every thing I do. Otherwise I couldn't find You at all, and this cannot be, since I can't possibly exist without You. Thus I must seek You in all things. If every day is "everyday," then every day is *Your* day, and every hour is the hour of Your grace.

Everything is "everyday" and Your day together. And thus, my God, I again understand something I have always known. A truth has again come to life in my heart, which my reason has already often told me—and of what value is a truth of reason when it is not also the life of the heart?

Again and again I must take out the old notebook in which I copied that short but vital passage from Ruysbroeck many years ago. I must reread it, so that my heart can regrasp it. I always find consolation in rediscovering how this truly pious man felt about his own life. And the fact that I still love these words after so many years of routine living is to me a sacred pledge that You will one day bless *my* ordinary actions too.

God comes to us continually, both directly and indirectly. He demands of us both work and pleasure, and wills that each should not be hindered, but rather strengthened, by the other. Thus the interior man possesses his life in both these ways, in activity and in rest. And he is whole and undivided in each of them, for he is entirely in God when he joyfully rests, and he is entirely in himself when he actively loves.

The interior man is constantly being challenged and admonished by God to renew both his rest and his work. Thus he finds justice; thus he makes his way to God with sincere love and everlasting works. He enters into God by means of the pleasure-giving tendency to eternal rest. And while he abides in God, still he goes out to all creatures in an all-embracing love, in virtue and justice. And that is the highest stage of the interior life.

Those who do not possess both rest and work in one and the same exercise, have not yet attained this kind of justice. No just man can be hindered in his interior recollection, for he recollects himself as much in pleasure as in activity. He is like a double mirror, reflecting images on both sides. In the higher part of his spirit he receives God together with all His gifts; in the lower he takes in corporeal images through his senses. . . .

I must learn to have both "everyday" and Your day in the same exercise. In devoting myself to the works of the world, I must learn to give myself to You, to possess You, the One and Only Thing, in everything. But how? Only through You, O God. Only through Your help can I be an "interior" man in the midst of my many and varied daily tasks. Only through You can I continue to be in myself with You, when I go out of myself to be with the things of the world.

It's not anxiety or non-being, not even death that can rescue me from being lost to the things of the world. Not the modern philosophers, but only Your love can save me, the love of You, who are the goal and attraction of all things. Only You are fulfillment and satiety, You who are sufficient even unto Yourself. It is only the love of You, my Infinite God, which pierces the very heart of all things, at the same time transcending them all and leaping upward into the endless reaches of Your Being, catching up all the lost things of earth and transforming them into a hymn of praise to Your Infinity.

Before You, all multiplicity becomes one; in You, all that has been scattered is reunited; in Your Love all that has been merely external is made again true and genuine. In Your Love all the diffusion of the day's chores comes home again to the evening of Your unity, which is eternal life.

This love, which can allow my daily routine to remain routine and still transform it into a home-coming to You, this love only You can give. So what should I say to You now, as I come to lay my everyday routine before You? There is only one thing I can beg for, and that is Your most ordinary and most exalted gift, the grace of Your Love.

Touch my heart with this grace, O Lord. When I reach out in joy or in sorrow for the things of this world, grant that through them I may know and love You, their Maker and final home. You who are Love itself, give me the grace of love, give me Yourself, so that all my days may finally empty into the one day of Your eternal Life.

CHAPTER VII

God of the Living

I should like to remember my dead to You, O Lord, all those who once belonged to me and have now left me. There are many of them, far too many to be taken in with one glance. If I am to pay my sad greeting to them all, I must rather travel back in memory over the entire route of my life's long journey.

When I look back in this way, I see my life as a long highway filled by a column of marching men. Every moment someone breaks out of the line and goes off silently, without a word or wave of farewell, to be swiftly enwrapped in the darkness of the night stretching out on both sides of the road. The number of marchers gets steadily smaller and smaller, for the new men coming up to fill the ranks are really not marching in my column at all.

True, there are many others who travel the same road, but only a few are traveling with me. For the only ones making this pilgrimage with me are those with whom I set out together, the ones who were with me at the very start of my journey to You, my God, the dear ones who were, and still are, close to my heart.

The others are mere companions of the road, who happen to be going the same way as I. Indeed there are many of them, and we all exchange greetings and help each other along. But the true procession of my life consists only of those bound together by real love, and this column grows ever shorter and more quiet, until one day I myself will have to break off from the line of march and leave without a word or wave of farewell, never more to return.

That's why my heart is now with them, with my loved ones who have taken their leave of me. There is no substitute for them; there are no others who can fill the vacancy when one of those whom I have really loved suddenly and unexpectedly departs and is with me no more. In true love no one can replace another, for true love loves the other person in that depth where he is uniquely and irreplaceably himself. And thus, as death has trodden roughly through my life, every one of the departed has taken a piece of my heart with him, and often enough my whole heart.

A strange thing happens to the man who really loves, for even before his own death his life becomes a life with the dead. Could a true lover ever forget his dead? When one has really loved, his forgetting is only apparent: he only *seems* to get over his grief. The quiet and composure he gradually regains are not a sign that things are as they were before, but a proof that his grief is ultimate and definitive. It shows that a piece of his own heart has really died and is now with the living dead. This is the real reason he can weep no more.

Thus I am living now with the dead, with those who have gone before me into the dark night of death, where no man can work. But how can I really live with the dead? How can I continue to find life in the one bond left between us, the bond of our mutual love? Deign to answer me, O God, for You have called Yourself the God of the living and not of the dead. How can I live with them?

Of what use is it to say, as do the philosophers, that the dead still exist, that they live on? Are they with *me*? Since I loved them and still love them, I must be with them. But are they also with me?

They have gone away; they are silent. Not a word comes through from them; not a single sign of their gentle love and kindness comes to warm my heart. How awfully still the dead are, how *dead!* Do they want me to forget them, as one forgets a fleeting acquaintance he made on a train, a stranger with whom he once exchanged a few friendly but meaningless words?

If it's true that those who have departed in Your love have not really lost their life, but have had it transformed into eternal, limitless, superabundant life, why then do I perceive no sign? Why are they for me as if they were no more? Is the eternal light into which they have entered —which is Your light, my God—so feeble that its rays can't reach down to me? Must not only their bodies, but also their love depart from me, in order to be with You?

My question thus turns away from them to You, my God, for You want Yourself to be called the God of the living and not of the dead.

But why am I asking this of You? You are as silent to me as my dead. I love You too, as I love my dead, the quiet and distant ones who have entered into night. And yet not even You give me answer, when my loving heart calls upon You for a sign that You and Your Love are present to me. So how can I complain about my dead, when their silence is only the echo of Yours? Or can it be that Your silence is Your answer to my complaint about theirs?

That must be the way it is, since You are the last answer, even though incomprehensible, to all the questions of my heart. I know why You are silent: Your silence is the framework of my faith, the boundless space where my love finds the strength to believe in Your Love.

If it were all perfectly evident to me here on earth, if Your Love of me were so manifest that I could ask no more anxious questions about it, if You had made absolutely crystal clear the most important thing about me, namely, that I am someone loved by You, how then could I prove the daring courage and fidelity of my love? How could I even have such love? How could I lift myself up in the ecstasy of faith and charity, and transport myself out of this world into Your world, into Your Heart?

Your Love has hidden itself in silence, so that my love can reveal itself in faith. You have left me, so that I can discover You. If You were with me, then in my search for You I should always discover only myself. But I must go out of myself, if I am to find You—and find You there, where You can be Yourself.

Since Your Love is infinite, it can abide only in Your Infinity; and since You will to manifest Your infinite Love to me, You have hidden it in my finiteness, where You issue Your call to me. My faith in You is nothing but the dark path in the night between the abandoned shack of my poor, dim earthly life and the brilliance of Your Eternity. And Your silence in this time of my prilgrimage is nothing but the earthly manifestation of the eternal word of Your Love.

That is how my dead imitate Your silence: they remain hidden from me because they have entered into Your Life. The words of their love no longer reach my ears, because they are conjoined with the jubilant song of Your endless Love. My dead live the unhampered and limitless Life that You live; they love with Your Love; and thus their life and their love no longer fit into the frail and narrow frame of my present existence. I live a dying life—*prolixitas mortis* is the Church's name for this life—so how can I expect to experience their eternal life, which knows no death?

And that is also the way they live for me. Their silence is their loudest call to me, because it is the echo of Your silence. Their voice speaks in unison with Yours, trying to make itself heard above the noisy tumult of our incessant activity, competing with the anxious protestations of mutual love with which we poor humans try to reassure each other. Against all this, their voice and Yours strive to enwrap us and all our words in Your eternal silence.

Thus Your word summons us to enter into Your Life. Thus You command us to abandon ourselves by the daring act of love which is faith, so that we may find our eternal home in Your Life. And thus I am called and commanded by the silence of my dead, who live Your Life and therefore speak Your word to me, the word of the God of Life, so far removed from my dying. They are silent because they live, just as we chatter so loudly to try to make ourselves forget that we are dying. Their silence is really their call to me, the assurance of their immortal love for me.

O silent God, God of the silent dead, living God of the living, who call to me through silence, O God of those who are silently summoning me to enter into Your Life, never let me forget my dead, my living. May my love and faithfulness to them be a pledge of my belief in You, the God of eternal life.

Let me not be deaf to the call of their silence, which is the surest and sincerest word of their love. May this word of theirs continue to accompany me, even after they have taken leave of me to enter into You, for thus their love comes all the closer to me. O my soul, never forget your dead, for they live. And the life they live, now unveiled in eternal light, is your own life, which will one day be revealed also in you.

O God of the living, may Your living not forget me, as I still walk in the valley of death. You have granted them everything, even Yourself; grant them this too, that their silence may become the most eloquent word of their love for me. May it lead me home to the Kingdom they now possess, to the life and light they now enjoy.

My waning life is becoming more and more a life with the dead. I live more and more with those who have gone before me into the dark night where no man can work. By Your life-giving grace, O Lord, let it become ever more a life of faith in Your light, shining now dimly in this earthly night. Let me live with the living who have preceded me in the sign of faith, who have gone before me into the bright day of eternal life, when no man need work, because You Yourself are this day, the Fullness of all Reality, the God of the Living.

When I pray, "Grant them eternal rest, O Lord, and let Thy perpetual light shine upon them," let my words be only the echo of the prayer of love that they themselves are speaking for me in the silence of eternity: "O Lord, grant unto him, whom we love in Your Love now as never before, grant unto him after his life's struggle Your eternal rest, and let Your perpetual light shine also upon him, as it does upon us."

O my soul, never forget the dead. O God of all the living, do not forget me, the dead one, but come one day to be my life, as You are theirs.

CHAPTER VIII

God of My Brothers

You have sent me to work among men, O God. You have laid the heavy burden of Your authority and Your sacred powers upon my shoulders, and bid me go out to Your creatures, whom You want to save. In a strict, almost brusque command, You have sent me away from Yourself, ordered me out among men.

Of course I had already spent most of my time associating with men anyway, even before Your word of consecration sent me out. I used to love it, to love and be loved, to be a close friend and to have close friends. It's an easy and very pleasant thing to be among men in this way. You visit only those you yourself have chosen, and stay as long as you please.

But now things are different. The men to whom I have been sent are of Your choosing, Lord, not mine. And I must be not their friend, but their servant. And when I get tired of them, it's not a sign that I should get up and leave, as it used to be, but rather a sign of Your command to stay.

O God, what strange creatures these men are, for whose

sake You have chased me away from You! For the most part they won't even listen to me when I come in Your name. They have absolutely no desire for Your grace and Your truth, the gifts You have given me to bring to them. And yet I must keep pounding on their doors again and again, like an unwanted but persistent peddler.

If I only knew that they were really rejecting You when they refuse to admit me, that would be some consolation. At least I wouldn't have to reproach myself for doing my job so badly. But as it is, I can't get rid of the agonizing thought that maybe even I would refuse to open the door, if someone came and knocked on it the way I do, claiming to be sent by You.

And even those who let me in don't treat me much better. They usually want everything but what I'm trying to bring. They want to tell me their little cares and worries; they want to pour out their hearts to me. And what a conglomeration comes spilling out! What a disheartening mixture of the comical and the tragic, of small truth and big lies, of little trials that are taken too seriously and big sins that are made light of!

And what do these men want of me? Sometimes it's material help, sometimes just the consolation of a sympathetic heart. Or if it's not that, then they look upon me as some kind of celestial insurance agent, with whom they can take out an accident policy for eternity, to make sure that You never break in upon their lives with the Omnipotence of Your Holiness and Justice. They want to sign a contract preventing You from ever shaking them out of their petty little weekday concerns and Sunday amusements, to bind You to an agreement whereby You'll leave them in peace, both in this life and in the next.

How seldom does anyone say, "Lord, what do You want me to do?" How rare it is that anyone really wants to hear the whole, unadulterated, and astounding message that we must love *You* passionately, and not ourselves, for *Your* sake, and not our own, and that we must *love* You, not just respect You and fear Your judgment. How seldom anyone wants to receive the gift of Your grace the way it really is: austere and plain, for Your honor, not just for our consolation, chaste and pure, silent and bold.

These are the men to whom You have sent me, and I cannot escape them. For their defects are not a signal to me to flee out of the land of the all-too-human, but rather a sign that I have really found the field in which You, O mysterious and extravagant God, want me to sow the seed of Your grace and Your truth, even with all its rocks and thorns and hard-trodden paths.

I must sow the seed and then watch how it falls by the wayside, upon the rocks, among thorns, how it is eaten by the birds of the air, all unfruitful. And even where it seems to fall upon good earth, it no sooner begins to spring up than it takes on the characteristics of the earth in which it took root, and thus is doomed to be blighted by petty human failings. The true fruit that it brings—thirty, sixty and a hundred-fold—only You seem to be able to see that. When I think I see it, I must still doubt, for haven't You Yourself said that none of us knows who is really worthy of Your Kingdom?

When I complain this way to You, about my brethren

63

to whom You have sent me, I don't mean to say that I am any better than they. I know my own heart, and You know it still better. It's no different from the hearts of the men I must approach in Your name.

When I complain to You of the heavy burden of my vocation, I know that I am acting exactly like those about whom I have just been complaining. I am acting like a small man who wants to be consoled, who is always thinking of his own sorrows, who can't for a minute forget his own troubles and his own comfort to lose himself in silent admiration of what a great thing it is to spend one's life in unselfishly serving You.

And that's just why it all looks so hopeless: haven't I enough burdens of my own to bear? Isn't my heart weak and miserable enough with its own troubles, without adding to it the crushing woes of others?

Or is that the very way my heart is meant to grow strong, by devoting itself patiently and uncomplainingly to the bearing of others' burdens? Do I regain my own inner strength precisely by being steadfast and courageous in the service of my brethren, and thereby giving testimony to the world that Your Heart is bigger than ours, that You are patient and long-suffering, that Your Mercy never disdains us, that Your Love is never outdone by our wretchedness? Is that the best way to take care of myself, by forgetting myself in the care of others?

If Your sending me out was an act of Your Mercy to me, O Lord—and how can I doubt that it was?—then it must be so. Then You must desire that I possess my own soul in patience, precisely through bearing in patience the souls of my brethren.

But look, my God, when I approach men with Your truth and Your grace—almost as if I were bringing them the last sacraments—when I knock on the door of their interior life and they let me in, they usually lead me only into the rooms in which they live their ordinary daily lives.

They tell me about themselves and their worldly affairs; they show me their poor earthly furniture. They talk a lot about trivialities, in order to stay away from the one subject that's really important. They try to make themselves and me forget why I have actually come, to bring You like the Blessed Sacrament into the inmost chamber of their hearts, where the eternal spark in them is sick unto death, where an altar to You should be erected, on which the candles of faith, hope, and love should be burning.

Instead of this, they receive me into the dingy rooms of their ordinary surface-life. These doors I have absolutely no trouble in opening. But I seek in vain for an entrance into the last depths where a man's eternal destiny is decided. In fact, it often seems to me that these men themselves have never found the door to that inner sanctuary where every man is sick unto death—or unto life. How then should I be able to find it?

Maybe it's all part of Your plan, that I never succeed in penetrating this door. Perhaps I am meant to be only an errand-boy who leaves Your gift and Your message at the delivery entrance, with no thought of being invited inside. Maybe it's just not my business to enter the interior castle of another's soul, to try to make sure that Your message and Your gift really become this man's eternal life through his freely given love.

Is that how it is? Do You want to be completely alone with the soul in this single decisive moment? Do you prefer to act alone in the center of a man's heart when he performs this all-important act? Is my task finished when I have "done my duty" and delivered my message? Can't I, or shouldn't I even try to carry You into the last depths of my fellow man, because You are already present there, just as You fill every part of whatever lives or exists, and are already present in every man to his eternal judgment or salvation?

But if you have commanded me really to care for souls, and not just to take care of my own "duty," then I must be able to penetrate into that hidden inner chamber. I must have some way of reaching the very center of their being, of touching the very tip of their soul. And if it's true that You alone have really found the way there, You with Your grace, against whose gentle omnipotence no heart succeeds in sealing itself off when You will to exercise Your mercy, then I am sure that You alone are the way I must go and the door through which I must pass, in order to find the soul of my brother.

I must find my way to You and penetrate ever more deeply into You, if I am not to be simply a more or less welcome guest, whom my fellow men put up with in the course of their daily routine. Only thus can I enter that last redoubt which is the abode of Your eternal light, or of eternal darkness.

No matter how hard men try to break off relations with You, You are always present to them. Even when they attempt to lock and bolt their souls against You, You are there at the very core of these futile efforts. You are present in Your unfathomable Love and Omnipotence, which hold sway even over the kingdom of every man's freedom. And thus it is that one who is entrusted with the help and care of souls can draw near to them only by drawing near to You, O King of all hearts.

So You haven't really sent me away from You, after all. When You assigned me the task of going out among men, You were only repeating to me Your one and only commandment: to find my way home to You in love. All care of souls is ultimately possible only in union with You, only in the love which binds me to You and thus makes me Your companion in finding a path to the hearts of men.

You are waiting to be found in love, and that which is the heart and soul of true love of You, prayer. If I had prayed more, I would be closer to souls. For prayer, when it is not just a begging for Your favors, enables me to grow in intimate, loving union with You. Thus it is not merely a useful aid in my work for souls, but the very first and last act of my apostolate.

Lord, teach me to pray and to love You. Then I shall forget my own wretchedness on account of You, for I shall be able to do the one thing that lets me forget it: patiently bear the poverty of my brethren into the land of

Your riches. Then, united with You, O God of my brothers, I shall really be able to be a brother to them. I shall be able to help them in the one thing that is really necessary: finding You.

CHAPTER IX

God of My Vocation

O God my Father, You are the God of free favors, of grace freely given. You show Your mercy to whomever You please, where and when You choose.

If it's true that Your calling of men to a share in Your own Life is a completely free gift, then, as I well understand, this summons is not something given to every man along with his nature. Man finds You only where You choose to be found.

And as proof that Your salvation is a gratuitous gift, every man's road to eternal life, even though it leads to Your Infinity which is everywhere, must still take the "detour" through that definite human being who was born in Palestine under Emperor Augustus and died under the Governor, Pontius Pilate. We must take the "indirect route" leading through Your Son who became man. Your grace comes to us not in the "always and everywhere" of Your all-pervasive Spirit, but in the "here and now" of Jesus Christ.

Your Holy Spirit blows where He will—where *He* will, not where I will. He is not simply always there, whenever and wherever a man wants Him to be. We must go to Him, there where He chooses to give His grace. And that's why your salvation is bound up with Your visible Church. That's why Your grace comes to us in visible signs.

This is all quite clear to me, Lord, and I'm very happy about this distinctive characteristic of Your grace. It's comforting to know that I can approach You not merely in the realm of "pure spirit"—this "pure spirit" about which the philosophers talk, when they start founding religions, has always struck me as being not spirit, but a pure ghost, anyway—but in concrete, tangible, visible signs. It warms my heart to know that I can be sure of Your power and presence in my life through the water of baptism, or by the audible word of forgiveness spoken by the priest, or in the holy bread of the altar.

For my part I want no religion of pure spirit, of pure internal experience. Basically, such a religion is a mere human invention, in which man ends up grasping only himself, instead of You. He plumbs only the shallow waters of his own spirit, and penetrates only his own poverty-stricken interior, instead of sounding the depths opened up by Your free word. And Your word tells us more of You than You could ever write in the narrow pages of Your creation.

But, my God, this arrangement of combined internal and external worship has brought something into my life which often lies heavily on my soul. You have made me Your priest, and have thus chosen me to be an earthly sign of Your grace to others. You have put Your grace into my hands, Your truth into my mouth. And although it

70

doesn't surprise me that men should recognize You when You come to meet them in Your only-begotten Son, or in the chaste water of baptism, or in the silent form of the host, or in the words of Scripture so simple and yet so profound, still I find it all but incredible that You desire to come into Your Kingdom in the hearts of men through *me*. How can men possibly recognize You in *me*?

Indeed You have gone so far as to give me, along with my priesthood, also all the other means You use to convey Your loving greeting to men. You have equipped me with Your word, Your truth, Your sacraments. And You have attached these things to my ministry in such a way that they penetrate into the inmost regions of free souls only when these souls accept *me*, only when they take *me* along in the bargain.

Can men really recognize You in me? Or can they at least grasp the fact that You have sent me as the ambassador of Your truth, the bearer of Your mercy? When this question occurs to me, it seems that Your Gospel of joy for my brethren is to me, the messenger, only a crushing burden.

I realize that You have sent me, that I am Your messenger—maybe a very pitiful one, but for all that still Your messenger, a man sent by You and stamped with Your ineffaceable seal. Your truth does not become false just because *I* preach it, even though I too am a sinful man, to whom the dictum can be applied: *omnis homo mendax,* "every man is a liar."

Your grace remains pure, even when it is dispensed through *my* hands. Your Gospel is still the good tidings of great joy, even when it's not particularly noticeable that *my* soul is exulting in God my Saviour. And Your light continues to shine forth, changing the dark death-shadows of our earth into the brilliant noonday of your grace, even when this light has to find its way to men through the cracked and dusty panes of *my* tiny lantern.

I know, Lord, that as a priest of Your true Church, I should not let the sense of my vocation, and the courage to preach Your Gospel in season and out of season, depend on the consciousness of my own personal worth. Your priest does not approach men as a revivalist or an enthusiast, not as a purveyor of mystic wisdom or gnostic or pentecostal prophet, or whatever else such men may call themselves. These men can communicate to others no more of You than they have themselves. But as a priest, I come as Your legate, as a messenger sent by Your Son, our Lord. And that is at the same time less and more, a thousand times more than anything else.

But, O God of my calling, it would be so much easier if I could just deliver Your message and then, when Your work is done, go back to living my own life. Then the burden of being Your messenger would be no heavier than that of any other messenger or administrator who does his job and is done with it. But Your charge to me, Your commission itself has become my very life. It ruthlessly claims all my energies for itself; it lives from my own life.

As your messenger, I can live my own personal life only by passing on Your word. I am Your messenger and nothing more. Your lamp—excuse me for being so bold,

Lord—burns with the oil of my life. In Your service there are no office hours after which a man can close up shop and be his own master again. I can never forget that I am Your servant and go back to being a mere "private citizen."

Truly it's an unspeakable honor and privilege to be able to serve You with all one's energy. I must thank You that You have turned my life to Your service, that I have no other "profession" than conveying the message of Your salvation. I must be eternally grateful that, in my life, profession and devotion are completely identical—there is no distinction between what I do out of duty and what I do out of love.

And yet, if it were only possible in Your service, as in every other, to separate official business from one's private life! How much easier it would be! And I don't say this because I would prefer to give You only a few hours' service a day, and spend more time communicating to others my own religious experiences and inspirations, setting them on fire with my own enthusiasm and conviction. On the contrary, I want to be *Your* messenger, the transmitter of *Your* truth and *Your* grace, and nothing more. And precisely because that's what I want, I sometimes wish that people could better distinguish my official position from my private life.

Can one pass on Your truth without having fully grasped it himself? Can I preach Your Gospel, if it has not struck deep roots in my own heart? Can I pass on Your Life, if I am not alive with it myself? Your holy signs can produce grace of their own power, it's true. But would my fellow men allow *me* to mark them with these signs, unless my own countenance were to them a sign that You had sent me? It's unavoidable: Your official business and my private life cannot be separated.

And that is precisely the burden of my life. For look, Lord: even when I announce Your pure truth, I'm still preaching my own narrowness and mediocrity along with it. I'm still presenting myself, the "average man." How can I bring my hearers to distinguish between You and me in the frightful mixture of You and me that I call my sermons? How can I teach them to take Your word to their hearts, and forget me, the preacher?

I want to be a transmitter of Your light, and to do so, I must nourish it with the oil of my life. And yet I can't avoid placing myself before the lantern, coming between Your light and the searching eyes of my fellow men. I seem to be good for nothing at all but making the already-dark shadows of this world even darker and longer.

I understand all too well that, at the end of my priestly life, I shall have been only Your poor, unprofitable servant. I shall have been the messenger whom You have sent on ahead, who, instead of clearing the way for You, more often succeeds only in being a roadblock. Any grace that goes out from me is *Your* grace. Whatever of mine goes out from me is nothing, only a hindrance or, at best, a means You employ to test my fellow men, to see whether their instinctive love can recognize You, even when You disguise Yourself, almost beyond all recognition, by appearing to them in me.

O God of my vocation, when I consider these things, I

must confess that I don't at all feel like taking my place in the proud ranks of Your confident and conquering apostles. I rather feel that I should be on my way, simply and humbly, walking in fear and trembling. I don't mean to criticize those among my brethren who can be so happily sure of themselves, those of Your servants who so unmistakably reflect the inner confidence that they are coming in the name of the Lord God of Hosts, and who are quite amazed if anyone does not immediately recognize in them the ambassadors of the Almighty.

I cannot belong to that fortunate group, O Lord. Grant me rather the grace to belong to the number of Your lowly servants who are rather amazed when they are received by their fellow men. Let my heart tremble again and again in grateful surprise at the miracles of Your grace, which is mighty in the midst of weakness. Let me continue to marvel that I meet so many men who allow me, poor sinner that I am, to enter into the secret chamber of their hearts, because they have been able to recognize You hidden in me.

Thus I shall be happy to set out again and again on my messenger's rounds to my fellow men. You have sent me, and so I go in Your name, not my own. Let Your power triumph through my weakness, whenever you desire it to do so.

As I proceed with Your message along the pathway of my life, I shall no doubt often experience what befell Your prophet of long ago: I shall be disillusioned with Jahweh, laughed to scorn by men, a man of contention before the whole world. Then I must speak out—and woe is me, if I do not—I must speak of You, the One whom it is more fitting to honor by silence. I must speak, even with the tormenting feeling of being mere sounding brass and tinkling cymbal. For who can really know for certain whether or not he possesses the love without which everything else is just hollow noise?

In the strength of Your word I shall march continually around the Jericho of men's souls, even with their laughter ringing in my ears, until You bring its walls crashing down. You will do this of Your own power, so that no man can boast before You of his prowess over souls. Thus will my mission be fulfilled, in the same way as was that of Your Son, my crucified Master. And for this, may You be praised for all eternity.

O God of my vocation, I am only a poor mask, behind which You have chosen to approach men as the hidden God. Grant me the grace day by day to be ever more free from sin and self-seeking. Even then I shall remain what I can't help being, Your disguise and Your unprofitable servant. But then at least I shall grow ever more like Your Son, who also had to envelop the eternal light of His divinity in the form of a servant, to be found in the garb and livery of a man.

When I bear the burden of Your calling, when Your mission weighs down heavily upon me, when Your Majesty humbles me, and my weakness is taken up into that of Your Son, then I may confidently trust that the hindrance which I have been to Your coming may still turn out to be a blessing to my brothers. Then perhaps You will transsubstantiate my servitude—for only You could work such a change, unseen by me and my fellow men—into a somehow sacramental form, under whose poverty You will be the bread of life for my brethren.

O God of my vocation, let my life be consumed as the Sacred Host, so that my brothers and I may live in You, and You in us, for all eternity.

CHAPTER X

God Who Is to Come

Every year Your Church celebrates the holy season of Advent, my God. Every year we pray those beautiful prayers of longing and waiting, and sing those lovely songs of hope and promise. Every year we roll up all our needs and yearnings and faithful expectation into one word: "Come!"

And yet, what a strange prayer this is! After all, You have already come and pitched Your tent among us. You have already shared our life with its little joys, its long days of tedious routine, its bitter end. Could we invite You to anything more than this with our "Come?" Could You approach any nearer to us than You did when You became the "Son of Man," when You adopted our ordinary little ways so thoroughly that it's almost hard for us to distinguish You from the rest of our fellow men?

In spite of all this we still pray: "Come." And this word issues as much from the depth of our hearts as it did long ago from the hearts of our forefathers, the kings and prophets who saw Your day still far off in the distance, and fervently blessed its coming. Is it true, then, that we only "celebrate" this season, or is it still really Advent?

Have You really already come? Was it really You, the God we were expecting when we poured forth our longing for "Him who was to come," for the Mighty God, Father of the Future, Prince of Peace, the God of Light and Truth and Eternal Happiness? Indeed, Your coming is promised in the very first pages of Holy Scripture, and yet on the last page, to which no more will ever be added, there still stands the prayer: "Come, Lord Jesus!"

Are You the eternal Advent? Are You He who is always still to come, but never arrives in such a way as to fulfill our expectations? Are You the infinitely distant One, who can never be reached? Are you the One toward whom all races and all ages, all the longings of all men's hearts must plod on eternally over never-ending highways?

Are You only the distant horizon surrounding the world of our deeds and sufferings, the horizon which, no matter where we roam, is always just as far away? Are You only the eternal Today, containing within itself all time and all change, equally near to everything, and thus also equally distant?

Is it that You don't want to come, because You still possess what we were yesterday and today are no more, and have already gone infinitely beyond what we shall be in the farthest future? When our bleeding feet have apparently covered a part of the distance to Your eternity, don't You always retreat twice as far away from us, into the immense reaches filled only by Your Infinite Being? Has mankind drawn the least bit closer to You in the thousands and thousands of years that have elapsed since it boldly began its most exciting and fearsome adventure, the search for You?

Have I come any nearer to You in the course of my life, or doesn't all the ground I have won only make my cup all the more bitter, because the distance to You is still infinite? Must we remain ever far from You, O God of Immensity, because You are ever near to us, and therefore have no need of "coming" to us? Is it because there is no place in Your world to which You must first "find Your way?"

You tell me that You have really already come, that Your name is Jesus, Son of Mary, and that I know in what place and at what time I can find You. That's all true, of course, Lord—but forgive me if I say that this coming of Yours seems to me more like a going, more like a departure than an arrival.

You have clothed Yourself in the form of a slave. You, the hidden God, have been found as one of us. You have quietly and inconspicuously taken Your place in our ranks and marched along with us. You have walked with us, even though we are beings who are never coming, but rather always going, since any goal we reach has only one purpose: to point beyond itself and lead us to the last goal, our end.

And thus we still cry: "Come! Come to us, You who never pass away, You whose day has no evening, whose reality knows no end! Come to us, because our march is only a procession to the grave." Despairing of ourselves, we call upon You—then most of all, when, in composure and quiet resignation, we bring ourselves to accept our finiteness.

We have called out to Your Infinity—Its coming is the sole hope we have of attaining unending life. For we have learned—at least those of us to whom you have granted the gift of knowing the final meaning of this life—that our search was in vain, that we were seeking the impossible. We had thought to escape by our own power from the strangling anxiety of being frail and transitory. We had hoped by a thousand different methods of our own clever devising to run away from our own being, and thus become masters of an eternal existence.

But bitter experience has taught us that we cannot help ourselves, that we are powerless to redeem ourselves from ourselves. And so we have called upon Your Reality and Your Truth; we have called down upon ourselves the Plenitude of Your Life. We have made appeal to Your Wisdom and Your Justice, Your Goodness and Your Mercy. We have summoned You, so that You Yourself might come and tear down the barriers of our finiteness, and turn our poverty into riches, our temporality into eternity.

You promised that You would come, and actually made good Your promise. But how, O Lord, how did You come? You did it by taking a human life as Your own. You became like us in everything: born of a woman, You suffered under Pontius Pilate, were crucified, died, and were buried. And thus You took up again the very thing we wanted to discard. You began what we thought would end with Your coming: our poor human kind of life, which is sheer frailty, finiteness, and death.

Contrary to all our fond hopes, you seized upon precisely this kind of human life and made it Your own. And You did this not in order to change or abolish it, not so that you could visibly and tangibly transform it, not to divinize it. You didn't even fill it to overflowing with the kind of goods that men are able to wrest from the small, rocky acre of their temporal life, and which they laboriously store away as their meager provision for eternity.

No, You took upon Yourself our kind of life, just as it is. You let it slip away from You, just as ours vanishes from us. You held on to it carefully, so that not a single drop of its torments would be spilled. You hoarded its every fleeting moment, so You could suffer through it all, right to the bitter end.

You too felt the inexorable wheel of blind, brute nature rolling over Your life, while the clear-seeing eye of human malice looked on in cruel satisfaction. And when Your humanity glanced upwards to the One who, in purest truth and deepest love, it called "Father," it too caught sight of the God whose ways are unfathomable and whose judgments are incomprehensible, who hands us the chalice or lets it pass, all according to His own holy Will. You too learned in the hard school of suffering that no "why" will ever ferret out the secret of that Will, which could have done otherwise, and yet chose to do something we would never understand.

You were supposed to come to redeem us from ourselves, and yet You, who alone are absolutely free and unbounded, were "made," even as we are. Of course, I know that You remained what You always were, but still, didn't our mortality make You shudder, You the Immortal God? Didn't You, the Broad and Limitless Being, shrink back in horror from our narrowness? Weren't You, Absolute Truth, revolted at our pretense?

Didn't You nail Yourself to the cross of creation, when You took as Your own life something which You had drawn out of nothing, when You assumed as Your very own the darkness that You had previously spread out in the eternal distance as the background to Your own inaccessible light? Isn't the Cross of Golgotha only the visible form of the cross You have prepared for Yourself, which towers throughout the spaces of eternity?

Is that Your real coming? Is that what mankind has been waiting for? Is that why men have made the whole of human history a single great Advent-choir, in which even the blasphemers take part—a single chant crying out for You and Your coming? Is Your humble human existence from Bethlehem to Calvary really the coming which was to redeem wretched mankind from its misery?

Is our grief taken from us, simply because You wept too? Is our surrender to finiteness no longer a terrible act of despair, simply because You also capitulated? Does our road, which doesn't want to end, have a happy ending despite itself, just because You are traveling it with us?

But how can this be? And why should it be? How can our life be the redemption of itself, simply because it has also become Your life? How can You buy us back from the Law, simply by having fallen under the Law Yourself (Gal. 4:5)?

Or is it this way: is my surrender to the crushing narrowness of earthly existence the beginning of my liberation from it, precisely because this surrender is my "Amen" to Your human life, my way of saying "Yes" to Your human coming, which happens in a manner so contrary to my expectations?

But of what value is it to me that my destiny is now a participation in Yours, if You have merely made mine Your own? Or have You made my life only the *beginning* of Your coming, only the starting point of Your life?

Slowly a light is beginning to dawn. I'm beginning to understand something I have known for a long time: You are still in the process of Your coming. Your appearance in the form of a slave was only the beginning of Your coming, a beginning in which You chose to redeem men by embracing the very slavery from which You were freeing them. And *You* can really achieve Your purpose in this paradoxical way, because the paths that *You* tread have a real ending, the narrow passes which *You* enter soon open out into broad liberty, the cross that *You* carry inevitably becomes a brilliant banner of triumph.

Actually You haven't come—You're still coming. From Your Incarnation to the end of this era is only an instant, even though millennia may elapse and, being blessed by You, pass on to become a small part of this instant. It is all only the one, single moment of Your single act, which catches up our destiny into Your own human life, and sweeps us along to our eternal home in the broad expanses of Your divine Life.

Since You have already begun this definitive deed, Your final action in this creation, nothing new can really happen any more. Our present era is the last: in the deepest roots of all things, time is already standing still. "The final age of the world has come upon us" (1 Cor. 10:11). There is only a single period left in this world: Your Advent. And when this last day comes to a close, then there will be no more time, but only You in Your Eternity.

If deeds measure time, and not time deeds—if one new event ushers in a new age, then a new age, and indeed the last, has dawned with Your Incarnation. For what could still happen, that this age does not already carry in its womb? That we should become partakers of Your Being? But that has already happened, the moment You deigned to become partaker of our humanity.

It is said that You will come again, and this is true. But the word *again* is misleading. It won't really be "another" coming, because You have never really gone away. In the human existence which You made Your own for all eternity, You have never left us.

But still You will come again, because the fact that You have already come must continue to be revealed ever more clearly. It will become progressively more manifest to the world that the heart of all things is already transformed, because You have taken them all to Your Heart.

You must continue to come more and more. What

86

has already taken place in the roots of all reality must be made more and more apparent. The false appearance of our world, the shabby pretense that it has not been liberated from finiteness through Your assuming finiteness into Your own life, must be more and more thoroughly rooted out and destroyed.

Behold, You come. And Your coming is neither past nor future, but the present, which has only to reach its fulfillment. Now it is still the one single hour of Your Advent, at the end of which we too shall have found out that You have really come.

O God who is to come, grant me the grace to live now, in the hour of Your Advent, in such a way that I may merit to live in You forever, in the blissful hour of Your Eternity.